LOVE FOR ANIMALS,
LARGE AND SMALL

Dedicated to all animals, large and small.

—Ingrid Newkirk

Table of Contents

Foreword by Bob Barker 1

Introduction 5

The Case That Started It All 9

Sheena's Long Journey Home 15

Thoroughbred Who Lost Every Race
    Finally Wins 21

The Liberation of Libby....................................24

A Beautiful Reflection 29

Blue's Clues Lead to a Horrifying Discovery—
    and a Miraculous Escape 33

Hot, Sick, and a Long Way from Home 37

Pulled out of the Trash, Her Name Was Meeka 41

Escape from an Unnatural Disaster...................45

No Milk for These Babies 49

The Chicken Who Was Left Behind 53

Seven Years a Slave...59

Life after Solitary Confinement 63

A Hollywood Ending for Bella and Edward 67

Ailing Pregnant Donkey Finds Room at the Inn 71

This Place Is the Pits 75

Rescuing a Hurricane's Forgotten Victims 79

A Kitten's Worst Nightmare 85

Changing Minds, Saving Lives..........................88

Epilogue 98

Foreword by Bob Barker

I've loved animals all my life, from the time I was a little boy playing with the dogs on the Sioux reservation in South Dakota. But it was my wife, Dorothy Jo, who made me realize that it's not enough just to love animals—we have to put that love into action. It was at her suggestion that we both became vegetarians way back in 1979. I've now been a vegetarian for over three decades, long enough to watch vegetarianism evolve from a "hippie" fad into a "hip" trend.

Dorothy Jo was ahead of her time (and even ahead of PETA's time!). When she died in 1981, I felt that the best tribute to her memory would be to keep up her work in behalf of animals, which included setting up a foundation in her name to fund spay/neuter programs and animal rescue. I started signing off every episode of *The Price Is Right* with a call for viewers to spay and neuter their dogs and cats. When I retired from *The Price Is Right* after 35 years, I asked the new host, Drew Carey, to continue my tradition, and he graciously agreed.

Perhaps it is because of my long show business career that I especially relate to the plight of animals in entertainment. One of my proudest achievements was helping to secure the freedom of three elephants —Iringa, Thika, and Toka—who had been held for decades in a cramped pen at the Toronto Zoo.

Because of Canada's cold climate (which is literally and figuratively a world away from the elephants' native African habitat), the elephants spent months at a time largely confined to a dark, depressing barn. Four elephants died at the zoo in as many years—but not one of old age.

Animal rights groups, including PETA, campaigned for years for the elephants to be sent to a sanctuary, and I wrote a letter to the Toronto City Council offering to cover the cost of transporting them to a new home. The city finally took me up on my offer and agreed to send them to the Performing Animal Welfare Society (PAWS), a California sanctuary, where they would have 85 acres to roam as well as a pond, heated barns, and even a Jacuzzi. It was the best money I ever spent.

I traveled to PAWS so that I could be there to see the elephants arrive, and it was quite a sight. Iringa and Toka, who were born in Africa, were unloaded first, and their joyful trumpeting as they explored their spacious new habitat brought tears to my eyes.

One of my other longtime causes is helping PETA free the bears held captive at three appalling roadside zoos on the Indian reservation in Cherokee, North Carolina. The bears at these zoos are confined to barren concrete pits and forced to beg tourists for food. One zoo employee even admitted to killing and eating one of the captive bears!

I personally visited Cherokee and met with tribal officials to plead for the bears' release, in addition to writing letters and essays, narrating a video exposé, and offering whatever assistance I could. Finally, after PETA conducted an undercover investigation at one of the zoos—Chief Saunooke Bear Park—the zoo was fined by the U.S. Department of Agriculture for violating the Animal Welfare Act, and its license was suspended. The zoo closed, and all the bears were sent to a sanctuary in Texas.

Victories like these—and the other ones mentioned in this book—make all the hard work pay off. I am so proud to have been a part of them, just as every other PETA supporter should be proud to have played a part in the rescue of thousands of animals over the years. Of course, much work remains to be done—two of the North Carolina bear pits are still operating, and my offer still stands to help pay for the relocation of another elephant at a Canadian zoo, Lucy, to a sanctuary. With the invaluable assistance of PETA supporters all over the world, I know that we will ultimately prevail.

Edmund Burke famously said, "All that is necessary for the triumph of evil is that good men do nothing." Fortunately, the good people at PETA always do something to defeat the evil directed at animals.

Introduction

It was just before lunchtime on Christmas morning when the call came in to the humane society. An injured stray dog was lying on the ice between two houses in Washington, D.C. Could we come and get her?

On that day, over 30 years ago, Washington was covered with a thick sheet of ice. Nothing moved. Nothing could move. We had a weather-imposed daylong curfew.

Well, most of us did. Some emergency services were in business. The humane society, where I worked at the time, was open because it had dogs and cats to feed and keep warm. Its volunteer drivers were on call, too, and I was one of them. My truck was out-fitted with studded snow tires and chains and 50-pound bags of sand. Just as PETA does now, the humane society always prided itself on getting to its destination at any time, day or night, even in adverse weather conditions.

When I got to the address, I managed to make my way slowly down ice-covered steps and across the skating-rink lawn to the caller's door. It was so cold that my fingers and feet were numb. Two men an-swered. A father and son? Behind them, in the warm, cozy room, I could see the Christmas tree and holiday lights. Music was playing. They pointed to the side of the house, shivered, and closed the door quickly.

The dog was lying on her side. A large German shepherd mix, she was so heavily pregnant that I was surprised she wasn't delivering the pups then and there. She tried to get away when she saw me coming. But her front legs had been crushed, and I could see broken bones protruding. She had apparently been hit by a car and managed to drag herself this far before collapsing. She was suffering from exposure and was wild-eyed with fear. Her only hope of getting away was to scramble past me, but her broken legs and the ice made escape impossible. I pulled out a long leash and put it around her neck.

Now I was faced with a dilemma. The dog and the litter she was carrying must have weighed over 70 pounds. She couldn't manage the walk—certainly not the steps to the sidewalk—under her own steam. I weighed in at about 115 pounds. Even on dry ground, picking her up would have been impossible. We were both shaking uncontrollably from the icy wind.

I blocked her escape route with two wooden pallets, anchored her to them, and gingerly maneuvered my way back to the house. Knock, knock. "Would anyone be able to help me get the dog up the steps to the truck?" I asked the beautifully dressed young woman who came to the door. The men on the couch shook their heads. No, that was my job. They weren't going out in that weather to touch some dirty mutt. No, thank you.

It took me awhile to administer the sedative to her, wait for its effects to kick in, and then to push and pull her body across the lawn and winch her, courtesy of a leash and the snow chains, up the steps to the truck. I have no recollection of how exactly I got her into the truck, but it wasn't easy. As I worked and she snored, I remember hearing Christmas music coming from inside the house.

There are some people who think that animal suffering isn't their business. But to paraphrase Charles Dickens, animalkind is our business. Or at least it should be.

A few years after this incident, I founded PETA on a principle that my mother taught me as a child: It doesn't matter who suffers but how. It doesn't matter how many legs the victim has or if the victim can speak our language or do advanced algebra. All that matters is the capacity for suffering. If a living being is in pain, we have an obligation to alleviate it and end it if we can.

The animals in this book were rescued because caring people didn't look the other way when they were faced with cruelty—they did something about it. They picked up the phone and called PETA. My heart is filled with gratitude for each person who has ever seen an animal who was being abused and said, "That's wrong. I'm going to get that stopped." That's the true meaning of "peace and goodwill to all."

Ingrid Newkirk
President
People for the Ethical Treatment of Animals

CHAPTER 1

SILVER SPRING
The Case That Started It All

When local police in Silver Spring, Maryland, raided a laboratory run by the Institute for Behavioral Research (IBR) in 1981, they opened not only a window on a shocking case of animal abuse but also the floodgates of public outrage over the plight of animals in laboratories. Tipped off by a PETA investigator who had been working at the lab for four months, the police confiscated 17 primates who became known as the "Silver Spring monkeys."

The 17 macaques—Adidas, Allen, Augustus, Big Boy, Billy, Brooks, Charlie, Chester, Domitian, Hard Times, Haydn, Montaigne, Nero, Paul, Sarah, Sisyphus, and Titus—were the survivors of an original group of 30 animals used by experimenter Edward Taub. Taub's experiments involved severing nerves in the monkeys' spines, arms, and legs and then tormenting them in an attempt to force them to use their injured limbs.

Before the investigator saw the monkeys, he heard their deafening screams. They were locked in barren cages less than 18 inches wide inside a windowless 15-foot-by-15-foot room. The cages were encrusted with filth, and the walls were spattered with blood and feces. Because no food bowls had been provided, the monkeys had to pick their food pellets out of pans of excrement beneath the wire cage bottoms. Feedings were sporadic, and the cages were never cleaned during the four months that PETA's investigator was there. The entire laboratory was littered with trash, rodent droppings, and dead cockroaches. The stench was overpowering.

Billy was a timid little fellow who had been deprived of the use of *both* of his arms. He was forced to push himself on his elbows across the wire cage grating and to eat his food by bending over and grasping it between his teeth, although they were painfully infected.

In one study, the experimenter forced the monkeys into a jury-rigged restraint chair in a dark, blood-spattered refrigerator for "noxious-stimuli experiments." He bound them with duct tape, burned them with a cigarette lighter, pinched their flesh (including their testicles) with surgical pliers, and administered electric shocks to "test" the feeling in their limbs. Taub's assistant said that some of the monkeys broke their arms trying to escape the shocks. Billy broke both of his useless arms in "accidents."

The stress and pain that the monkeys endured caused most of them to become neurotic, spinning in their cages and mutilating their own bodies, including chewing off their own fingers and toes. They also injured their deadened limbs accidentally, sometimes catching and then tearing off their fingers on the jagged, broken, and rusted wires that protruded from the cages. (Police documented that 39 of the fingers on the monkeys' hands were severely deformed or missing.) Their wounds were never treated by a veterinarian.

PETA's investigator found a freezer containing the remains of two monkeys and was told that one, Caligula, had died after mutilating his own chest cavity during an acute pain test. The investigator also found other dead monkeys who had been dumped into a barrel of auto parts.

Despite having no previous experience working in a laboratory, PETA's investigator was put in charge of one test in which he was told to starve the monkeys for several days and then taunt them with handfuls of food and videotape their frustrated reactions. Taub told him simply to look for something "interesting." (The investigator sneaked food to the animals but didn't think that would "interest" Taub.)

To bolster PETA's case, the investigator secretly took five medical and primate experts into the laboratory late at night. All filed affidavits condemning the facility's condition and procedures. Veterinarian and syndicated columnist Dr. Michael Fox wrote, "It is my professional opinion that the monkeys … were, without exception, suffering unnecessarily."

Armed with those affidavits and his own notes and photos, PETA's investigator went to the police. After a judge issued a search-and-seizure warrant, the authorities raided the lab and confiscated the monkeys.

"It was absolutely filthy, just incredibly dirty, like nothing I've ever been in. I've executed lots and lots of search warrants," said the officer who led the raid. "I've worked in murder, in narcotics, in vice, but this was the first time I went into a room and I felt legitimately concerned for my health just being there."

The monkeys were in awful shape. Many had open, festering wounds, and much of their once-lustrous hair was missing. Their tails were bald because of malnutrition, and they had pulled out clumps of fur on their arms and legs out of frustration, anger, and fear. After years of confinement to cages barely larger than their own bodies, they were frail and frightened. Once outside, they stared up anxiously at the crowds of uniformed officers and the media, almost blinded by the sunlight they had not seen since the day they were snatched from their home in the Philippines many years earlier.

For a week and a half, they received proper food, room to exercise, and toys to play with in the home of a PETA supporter, but the monkeys' respite was short-lived. Shockingly, the judge gave Taub custody of the monkeys even though he had been charged with 17 counts of cruelty. Meanwhile, the National Institutes of Health (NIH), which funded Taub's experiments, suspended his grant and began its own investigation.

Five days after being returned to the lab, Charlie died of what Taub called a "heart attack." That senseless death helped to persuade the judge to remove the monkeys from IBR. Taken to an NIH primate facility in Maryland, Hard Times was soon euthanized because of paralysis from the neck down.

In a landmark decision, Taub was convicted of six counts of cruelty for failure to provide proper veterinary care. It was the first time in U.S. history that a federally funded animal experimenter had been convicted of cruelty.

Taub appealed, and his conviction was overturned on a technicality—the court ruled that because he received federal funding, Taub didn't have to obey state anti-cruelty laws. Nevertheless, NIH terminated Taub's grant and the IBR lab closed. But even though NIH said it had no further use for the monkeys, it refused to release them to a sanctuary.

PETA repeatedly filed for custody, but we were rejected on the grounds that we didn't have proper legal "standing." The case ultimately went all the way to the U.S. Supreme Court, which ruled in PETA's favor and sent the case back to a lower court.

While the case wound its way through the courts for more than a decade, PETA turned to Congress for help and received it in the form of both a letter of recommendation for the monkeys' freedom signed by over 300 representatives and senators and a bill introduced by then-Rep. Bob Smith that would order NIH to release the monkeys to a sanctuary. Despite having more than 130 cosponsors, the bill never got a hearing.

Without any warning, the monkeys were secretly sent to a primate research center in Louisiana, where Brooks died after choking on his own vomit while being force-fed. In 1987, the five surviving "control" monkeys who had not been surgically crippled—

Adidas, Chester, Haydn, Montaigne, and Sisyphus—
were sent to the San Diego Zoo. For the first time
in years, they were able to go outdoors, bask in the
sun, eat fresh fruit, and sleep on soft bedding. The
monkeys who remained in Louisiana were ultimately
experimented on and euthanized.

The Silver Spring monkeys case was historic. It
led to the nation's first arrest and criminal conviction
of an animal experimenter for cruelty to animals, the
first confiscation of abused animals from a laboratory, and the first U.S. Supreme Court victory for
animals used in experiments.

It prompted landmark changes to the federal
Animal Welfare Act and renewed public scrutiny of
animal experiments. When PETA was founded, the
cosmetics industry insisted that animal tests were
indispensable. Today, more than 1,500 companies
refuse to test their products on animals, cosmetics
tests on animals have even been banned in several
countries, and many forward-thinking scientists are
using sophisticated non-animal methods to study
diseases and lifesaving surgical techniques.

CHAPTER 2

Sheena

Sheena's Long Journey Home

S heena knew something was wrong the second
Gayle closed the car door. Usually, rides meant
adventures—maybe a trip to the park or a
friend's house—but this time, something was different.

She paced in the backseat, glancing from window
to window for any clue as to where they were going.
Finally, they pulled up outside an unfamiliar building, and Gayle parked the car. As soon as the engine
went quiet, Sheena's ears perked up. Dogs—dozens
and dozens, probably—were barking inside. Some
howled a low, mournful song. Sheena began to pant
nervously as Gayle led her toward the building.
What was this place?

Inside, Gayle talked to a person behind a desk,
signed some papers, and then crouched down in
front of Sheena and said goodbye. She handed
Sheena's leash to a stranger and was gone.

Week after week, Sheena peered out from behind
the bars of her cage, hoping that Gayle would come
back. Sometimes Gayle visited to check on her, and
Sheena would be beside herself with joy. But Gayle
always left again, and Sheena began to lose hope.
Then one day, someone took her out of her cage and
out of the shelter. Was she finally going home?

No, this place wasn't anything like home. Sheena found herself in another cage—this time, in a laboratory at the University of Utah (the U), along with dozens of other terrified animals.

When PETA investigated the U in 2009, we learned that the school obtained many of its victims from animal shelters because of an appalling state "pound-seizure" law that required shelters in Utah to sell animals to laboratories upon request. Hundreds of homeless cats and dogs like Sheena had been tortured in invasive, painful, and often deadly experiments.

Among these animals was a pregnant cat who had been obtained from the Davis County animal shelter. She gave birth to eight kittens the same day she arrived at the U's laboratories. When the kittens were just 7 days old, experimenters injected a chemical into their brains to cause fluid to build up. After the surgery, the distressed mother cat—who had tenderly cared for her kittens before they were taken away for the experiment—seemed to sense that there was something very wrong with the kittens and stopped nursing them. They all died.

Another animal who ended up at the U was Robert, a friendly, gentle orange-and-white tabby cat. The U bought Robert from the Davis County animal shelter for $15 and renamed him F09-017. Experimenters cut into Robert's skull to implant electrodes in his brain, leaving a large gash running from his forehead back past his ears. Then they put him through a series of experiments in which current was fired through the electrodes, stimulating nerves that caused Robert's legs to move involuntarily. After each experiment, Robert was tired and groggy, his pupils were dilated, his eyes were glassy, and he vomited repeatedly. Over time, this affectionate cat became skittish and withdrawn.

Mice and rats at the U developed enormous tumors and were infected with painful, deadly illnesses. Rats and monkeys had holes drilled into their skulls in invasive brain experiments. The monkeys were kept in solitary confinement in steel cages and kept constantly thirsty so that they would do whatever experimenters wanted in exchange for a sip of water. During experimental sessions, they were strapped into restraints that resembled electric chairs.

Sheena was slated to be tortured in similar experiments. But when Gayle called the North Utah Valley Animal Shelter to check on her and learned that she had been sold to the U, Gayle immediately called PETA's emergency hotline for help.

With advice from PETA, Gayle contacted the U and insisted that it return Sheena to her. Miraculously, the school agreed to do so. Just in time for Christmas, PETA helped Gayle find Sheena a loving foster home. Safe at last, Sheena dropped to the ground and rolled gleefully on her back in the fresh snow, all four feet kicking up in the air at once.

After PETA released the findings of our shocking investigation, Robert was also rescued from the U's laboratories, rehabilitated, and put up for adoption. The U was cited for federal Animal Welfare Act violations, and Utah legislators voted by an overwhelming majority to amend the state's pound-seizure law, making it optional for animal shelters to sell dogs and cats to laboratories for experiments. Almost immediately after the law took effect, Davis County announced that it would no longer sell animals to laboratories. Months later, the U announced that it would no longer obtain animals from shelters.

Homeless animals in Utah like Sheena and Robert will never again be betrayed by the shelters that are supposed to keep them safe, but work continues in order to protect animals in other states where pound seizure remains legal. We won't give up until every cage is empty.

Our task must be to free ourselves… by widening our circle of compassion to embrace all living creatures and the whole of nature and its beauty.

—Albert Einstein

CHAPTER 3

Coming Home

Thoroughbred Who Lost Every Race Finally Wins

Coming Home's life started out with great promise. She is the granddaughter of Kentucky Derby winner Unbridled—an impressive pedigree. But perhaps as a sign of impending doom, she is also a cousin of Eight Belles, the filly who was euthanized after tragically shattering both front ankles in the 2008 Derby.

When PETA's investigator first spotted her, Coming Home, who had been used for racing, was huddled in the corner of a pen at a horse auction in Ohio. She was painfully thin, and thick, yellowish fluid oozed from her eyes and nose. Every once in a while, one of the other horses in the pen would lash out at her in fear, and as a result, she was covered with wounds from being bitten and kicked.

When it came time for her to be auctioned off, Coming Home was herded into the arena by shouting men cracking whips. Terrified, she made several attempts to bolt, but it was no use—there was no escape. As she shifted nervously from foot to foot, the auctioneer kept up a running stream of patter that sounded like gibberish to her. She had no way of knowing that her life was about to take a horrifying turn for the worse: She was sold to a slaughterhouse "kill buyer" for $200.

Coming Home was herded into a holding pen that was so crowded, she could barely move, and other frightened, doomed horses kept kicking and biting her. She was just hours away from being sent to slaughter when a PETA undercover investigator stepped in and rescued her.

Like other Thoroughbreds, Coming Home had started racing when her skeletal system was still growing and unprepared to handle the pressures of running on a hard track at high speeds. Many of the horses at her stable were given drugs—both legal and illegal—that masked pain, enabling them to run with injuries when they should have been resting and healing. Racing young horses and drugging them often leads to catastrophic breakdowns like the one that happened to Eight Belles. One study on racetrack injuries concluded that out of every 22 races, one horse sustains an injury bad enough to prevent him or her from finishing the race, while another study estimates that 800 Thoroughbreds per year die in North America from racing injuries.

Coming Home was lucky in that she didn't sustain a catastrophic injury that would have called for her to be euthanized right on the track like her cousin, but at age 6, despite her promising pedigree, she had never won a single race. She was, in horse-racing parlance, a "rat," or a horse who doesn't make money. So she had to go. She became one of the approximately 10,000 cast-off Thoroughbreds sent to Canada, to Mexico, and overseas every year to be slaughtered.

Yet even if she had been a champion, Coming Home still may not have been safe. Former Kentucky Derby winner Ferdinand was slaughtered after being sold to a Japanese breeding farm and failing to sire winning offspring. Exceller, a million-dollar horse who was inducted into the National Racing Museum's Hall of Fame, was killed at a Swedish slaughterhouse.

But thanks to the support of generous PETA members, who make our investigations possible, Coming Home beat the odds. She has finally come home. Today, she lives on a spacious ranch in New Mexico, where she runs with other horses, her head once again held high. Even though she never won a race, in the eyes of her adoring human family, she's a champion. She even has a new name to fit her new position in life: Little Winner.

CHAPTER 4

LIBBY

The Liberation of Libby

She didn't have a name, only a number tattooed inside her ear: 534120. Bone-thin, full of worms, and suffering from severely rotted teeth, the little brown dog was so terrified that she crawled on her stomach instead of walking, the whites of her eyes flashing with fear.

For much of her life, her world consisted of little more than the cold concrete floor of a kennel, the sting of chemicals on her skin, and the harsh voices of her captors screaming at her. Number 534120 was one of nearly 250 animals who were rescued from a hellish laboratory in North Carolina called Professional Laboratory and Research Services, Inc. (PLRS), following a nine-month PETA investigation.

The laboratory intentionally infested dogs, cats, and rabbits with worms, fleas, and ticks and then force-fed them experimental compounds or smeared their skin with toxic insecticides. In one test commissioned by a corporation whose products are sold in grocery stores and drugstores, a chemical was applied to the necks of 57 cats. The cats immediately had seizures, foamed at the mouth, lost their vision, and bled from their noses. Despite this, these traumatized animals had the substance smeared on them a second time the very same day.

As if being used as a living test tube weren't cruel

enough, the animals were verbally and physically abused on a regular basis by the laboratory workers, who seemed to despise them—and PETA's investigator caught it all on camera.

Employees swore at animals and screamed in their faces. Dogs and cats who were too frightened to walk were often kicked, thrown, dragged, and lifted by their throats. Many dogs were covered with raw, oozing sores from being forced to live in pools of their own urine and feces. On the rare occasions that the cages were cleaned, workers blasted them with high-pressure hoses, bleach, and other harsh chemicals while they were still inside, leaving them drenched and shivering.

Animals were deprived of veterinary care for bloody feces, worm infestations, oozing sores, abscessed teeth, hematomas, and pus- and blood-filled infections. One PLRS worker used pliers to pull the teeth of a dog who hadn't been properly anesthetized and was trembling and twitching in pain. Another worker maliciously tried to rip out a cat's nails by shoving her into a wire fence so that she would cling to it with her claws and then wrenching her off.

The daily abuse that our investigator recorded in her log notes is the stuff of nightmares:

> I witnessed [a supervisor] grab a cat, who had escaped from a cage, by his or her head. The cat then screamed and [the supervisor] tossed the cat back into the cage. [The supervisor] said, "Get your ass in there" and "You

25

are working" to the cat. She tossed the cat hard enough that I heard a "bang" sound when the cat hit the back of the cage.

While weighing cats in room 28, I witnessed [another senior caretaker] slap a cat on the head because the cat had scratched her on the back while she was holding him/her. ... After this incident, [she] appeared to be upset, as she was cursing and threw several cats about 3' through the air against the back of runs which confine them. The impacts were hard enough that a couple of cats lost their footing and landed on their sides/back when they hit the floor. ... I witnessed [a senior caretaker] pull a cat—who had escaped from her grip —by the tail for approximately 10' while trying to catch him/her.

Prior to clocking in, [an employee] said that she was surprised that PLRS [had] put so many of the dogs "down." She said that she was happy that they [had] "killed" Brutus, because he was one of the dogs who jump[ed] on her and, as she said, "I hate him." When I asked her how she prevented him from jumping on her, she said, "I smacked him."

Just one week after PETA released the results of our investigation and filed a complaint with the U.S. Department of Agriculture, the laboratory shut its doors and surrendered more than 50 cats and nearly 200 dogs. PLRS was cited for dozens of violations of federal animal-welfare laws, and a grand jury indicted four PLRS workers on 14 felony cruelty-to-animals charges—the first time in U.S. history that laboratory workers faced felony charges for their abuse and neglect of animals in a laboratory. Neither number 534120 nor any other animal will ever again be tormented by PLRS.

Today, 534120 is called Libby, and it's not just her name that's different. She walks with her head held high, filled with *joie de vivre*. She loves to race, wrestle, and play tug-of-war with her canine buddies. Imprisonment in a lonely laboratory cage has been replaced by long walks in the mountains, where she darts up and down the trails, her tail whipping wildly the whole time. Instead of sleeping on the cold, hard concrete, she snuggles under the covers at night with her loving guardian and canine "siblings." She will never again be just a number.

CHAPTER 5

BEN

A Beautiful Reflection

L ooking into Ben's eyes was like looking down into an abyss. There was nothing but infinite despair reflected in them.

Ben the bear had been confined for six lonely years to a small concrete cell in a North Carolina roadside zoo called Jambbas Ranch Tours. He could only pace endlessly—a few steps one way, then a few steps back, over and over again. He stared listlessly at the world outside his four chain-link walls—a big, wide world that must have seemed so tantalizingly close yet beyond his grasp.

In his natural forest home, Ben would have been constantly on the move, roaming for miles through forests and meadows. He would have taken delight in discovering tasty treats such as wild blueberries, napping in soft nests of leaves, splashing in mountain streams, and finding a cozy den in which to hibernate.

Ben had none of those things in his kennel-like cage. Instead, he had a concrete floor—without even so much as a blade of grass. His tiny sleeping hut didn't even have a door. He couldn't get a moment away from prying human eyes, much less hibernate as bears need to do.

Although bears love to swim, Ben wasn't even provided with a plastic kiddie pool in which to cool off. In a poignant act of desperation, he would some-times attempt to beat the muggy Southern heat by stepping into his drinking trough. Of course, it was way too small to hold him, much less cool him, and all he succeeded in doing was making his water filthy and undrinkable.

Bears like Ben eat a wide variety of vegetation, fish, and fruit. At Jambbas, Ben was given cheap dog food. To add insult to injury, the kibble was simply dumped onto the floor of his cage, right where he had to urinate and defecate.

During the six years in his prison cell, Ben had paced an infinite number of steps, so many that the pads of his feet had worn thin and you could see the pink of his soft flesh peeking out. The despondent bear would futilely push and bite at the chain-link fence and would reach out underneath it as if trying to grab the freedom he longed for.

PETA knew we had to get Ben out of there, so we joined forces with concerned North Carolina citizens and the Animal Legal Defense Fund and filed a law-suit to free him. Appalled by Ben's living conditions, the judge ruled that they violated state laws, stating that confining Ben to a cramped kennel was "the functional equivalent to forcing a human to live in a small closet."

The judge also declared that Jambbas had caused Ben "unjustifiable physical and psychological suffer-ing" and awarded permanent custody of Ben to the Performing Animal Welfare Society (PAWS), which operates a sanctuary in California.

Ben must have wondered what was happening when he was let out of his cage for the first time in years and loaded onto "Bear Force One"—a climate-controlled cargo plane loaned by FedEx for the flight to the PAWS sanctuary. Was this really happening? Was he really free?

Upon arrival, Ben pawed the earth and sniffed the grass as if he couldn't believe it was real. Within minutes, he had climbed into his very own pool and begun splashing the water with his paws like an exuberant kid. No more jamming himself into his water bowl—this was living!

Now, Ben spends his days in a lush, forested habitat, stopping for the occasional back scratch on a favorite tree. He naps peacefully in his large straw nest under the oak trees.

Today, there is no vacant, listless stare. Instead, Ben's eyes sparkle and shine with intelligence and curiosity. He has emerged from his shell and become active and interested in everything around him. Ben is a bear again.

CHAPTER 6

BLUE

Blue's Clues Lead to a Horrifying Discovery—and a Miraculous Escape

During the cold winter months, when wind, rain, hail, and snow dominate the weather forecast in southeastern Virginia and northeastern North Carolina, PETA staffers and volunteers spend every weekend delivering straw bedding and doghouses to dogs in need. In these pockets of deep poverty near PETA's headquarters at the Sam Simon Center in Norfolk, Virginia, people often have trouble paying their heating bills, and dogs who are left outside have no warmth at all.

PETA's straw-delivery volunteers see the worst that society has to offer—dogs starved for attention (and often for food, too), sentenced to life on a chain or in a cramped pen, and surrounded by mud and garbage. Other dogs have nothing more than old refrigerators, truck camper shells, or overturned barrels for "shelter"—if they have any at all, even during snowstorms. Some dogs suffer from heartworm disease, flystrike so severe that pieces of their ears have been eaten away, frostbite, broken bones, mange, and enormous, oozing tumors—all left untreated.

Even so, PETA's staffers and volunteers still encounter situations that shock them, and that's what happened in Portsmouth, Virginia, one cold February day.

The volunteers were chatting with one man, asking if he knew of anyone in the area whose dog might be in need of straw bedding or a doghouse, when they spotted a plastic dog crate behind a house across the street. The carrier was old, battered, and dirty. Because it was surrounded by garbage, the volunteers thought at first that the carrier had been junked and set out for trash collection.

Then they heard it: thump, thump, thump. It was the unmistakable sound of a wagging tail beating against the carrier's sides. There was a dog in there! As the volunteers got closer, the dog in the carrier grew increasingly animated, hoping against hope that someone had come to his rescue at last. He began barking, jumping up and down, and pawing frantically at the carrier door in excitement.

It was then that the volunteers realized that the dog wasn't alone. There was a second dog in the carrier, but she wasn't barking or wagging her tail.

That dog, a pit bull named Dynasty, was lying on her side, motionless, not reacting in any way, even though the other dog was stepping on her in his excitement. The volunteers realized, with sinking hearts, that she was dead. They were stunned at how emaciated she was: Her hips, ribs, and spine jutted out in sharp relief against her brindle fur. One of her hind legs was lying at an odd angle, too.

The surviving dog, a black-and-white pit bull mix named Blue because of his vivid periwinkle eyes, was also malnourished, and his white paws were stained yellow from having to stand in his own urine. The volunteers were told that the two dogs had been shoved into that crate so that they would be out of the way for a birthday party. One wouldn't want to upset the guests, after all. Then the dogs were simply forgotten.

The PETA volunteers called the police, and after the responding officer assessed the situation, he turned Blue as well as Dynasty's remains over to PETA.

An examination by our veterinarian revealed that Dynasty didn't have a single ounce of fat on her body and had been suffering from an untreated broken leg. The only contents of her stomach were a few wisps of straw bedding that she had eaten out of sheer desperation.

After a judge heard testimony from PETA and a veterinarian with a local SPCA, the dogs' owner was found guilty of cruelty to animals, convicted of starving Dynasty to death and depriving her of veterinary treatment. The horrified judge said that he wished he could impose on the owner a sentence similar to the one imposed on Dynasty and Blue—confining him to a crate without food or water in the middle of winter—but, he said, that would amount to "cruel and unusual punishment."

As for Blue, his darkest days are behind him. He was adopted into a loving home where he never has to worry about going hungry again. In honor of Blue's "adoptaversary," his new guardians threw a party, complete with balloons, cupcakes, and human and canine guests. This time, instead of having to listen to the revelry from outdoors in a cold, lonely crate, Blue was the guest of honor.

CHAPTER 7

Alaska

Hot, Sick, and a Long Way from Home

I t's a no-brainer. Polar bears belong at the North Pole. Their bodies are perfectly adapted to living in subfreezing temperatures and traveling over vast expanses of snow and ice. So who in their right mind would ever dream of sending a group of polar bears to the tropics to perform circus tricks? Well, that's exactly what the Mexico-based Suarez Bros. Circus did.

For years, the circus imprisoned a polar bear named Alaska and seven others in cages no larger than 64 square feet and dragged them around the Caribbean and Central and South America in swelteringly hot weather, forcing them to perform silly tricks.

Alaska and the other bears spent their days lying in their own waste in their cramped transport cages, panting in the tropical heat. Driven mad by the confinement, they swayed back and forth constantly in a vain attempt to comfort themselves. Biologists call this "zoochosis," or captivity-induced mental illness. It's common in animals in zoos and circuses, especially bears, who roam enormous territories in their natural habitat.

Even though polar bears normally spend much of their time in the water, Alaska and the others had no access to pools for swimming or providing any relief from the relentless heat. Some days, the temperature skyrocketed to 113 degrees Fahrenheit. The bears, in their thick fur coats, must have felt as if they were being roasted over hot coals.

Because Alaska and the others were so miserable and physical exertion just made them feel hotter, they were often reluctant to move. All they wanted was to be left alone.

But the show must go on, as they say, and if the bears weren't in the mood to put on a show, too bad—the man holding the whip or stick would smack them across their backs or legs or even slap them in the face to make them perch on podiums, slip down a slide, walk on their hind legs, and perform other pointless tricks.

Some of the bears were afraid to climb up the stairs of the slide, so the man would hit them with the whip as loud music played gaily in the background. When a bear finally got to the top and pitched headlong down the slide, the crowd laughed and cheered, oblivious to the fear and misery.

Some of the bears became ill and so emaciated that their hip bones protruded. Others suffered from a skin disease. Because the bears could never bathe, their fur grew dirty, lank, and matted. They were also exposed to dangers that they would never have encountered in their natural habitat.

One bear was coughing and had difficulty breathing. He stopped eating and grew tired and weak. He was diagnosed with heartworms, which come from mosquitoes, something bears never have to worry about in the Arctic. Untreated, his condition deteriorated for months until he eventually died of congestive heart failure.

While the circus was performing in Puerto Rico, the Puerto Rican Department of Natural and Environmental Resources charged it with cruelty, based on a PETA complaint that the bears were living in filthy cages with no relief from the heat. Incredibly, the circus was found not guilty.

Undeterred, PETA, joined by several other groups and individuals, filed a lawsuit against the U.S. Department of Agriculture and the U.S. Department of the Interior alleging that granting a permit to import the bears into Puerto Rico (a U.S. territory) violated the Marine Mammal Protection Act. The federal Marine Mammal Commission, in responding to a videotape taken by rangers with the Puerto Rican Department of Natural and Environmental Resources showing the bears swaying neurotically in their pitiful cages, called for an interagency evaluation. Canadian officials were so horrified to learn that the bears, some of whom had been captured in the Canadian wilderness, had wound up in such hellish conditions that Manitoba strengthened its rules governing polar-bear exportation.

In the meantime, the bears' backgrounds were called into question, and evidence was found indicating that Alaska may not have been born at Zoo Atlanta, as the circus had claimed on her import application. After we reported our suspicions to the

U.S. Fish & Wildlife Service (FWS), the agency used DNA testing to prove conclusively that Alaska's identity had been "stolen," a violation of federal law. The FWS confiscated Alaska and sent her to the Baltimore Zoo (now The Maryland Zoo in Baltimore) to be a companion for the zoo's formerly solitary polar bear, Magnet.

When Alaska first arrived at the zoo, she was sick, lethargic, filthy, and, her caretakers soon discovered, deaf. While she was still in her quarantine room, Magnet made a gentle overture of friendship—he presented her with several sticks as "gifts." She "thanked" him by nibbling on his toes through the bars of her cage door. Soon, they were splashing and playing together in a cool, refreshing pool, the first time Alaska had been able to dip her toes in water in years. Rancid scraps were replaced with wholesome, healthy food. There were no more frightening and confusing tricks. Alaska's battered body and broken spirit began to heal.

Within a year, the rest of the polar bears had been rescued as well—all but poor 18-year-old Royal, whose body just gave out on his way to freedom. But Boris, Kenneth, Barle, Wilhelm, and Marsha were all flown to zoos in states with more suitable climates. Soon, their years in a tropical hell had faded to a distant nightmare.

CHAPTER 8

Meeka

Pulled out of the Trash, Her Name Was Meeka

The first thing that struck her was the odor— the sickening smell of the accumulated waste of tens of thousands of animals.

That's what PETA's investigator encountered as she began her first shift at Rainbow World Exotics, a Texas breeding mill that supplied birds, rabbits, guinea pigs, and other small, vulnerable animals to pet stores such as PetSmart and Petco.

But there was more. Untreated illnesses. Neglect. Crude surgeries performed by untrained staff. Severely crowded enclosures. These were just some of the horrific, nightmarish conditions that the investigator found at Rainbow World Exotics.

But what continues to haunt her to this day is the memory of the littlest of animals, the hamsters, rats, and mice, who were dumped into trash cans while still alive, as if their lives meant nothing. As if they were garbage.

In the trash or near it is where the investigator found Meeka, Trey, and three other hamsters.

A worker had thrown Meeka more than 5 feet in the direction of a trash barrel. But she had fallen just short and landed hard on the concrete floor. The little hamster was lying there, helpless, next to the trash can when PETA's investigator scooped her up so that she wouldn't be trampled to death by careless employees.

She found Trey, Lily, Rusty, and Colt moving around in a bin that was filled with feces, urine-soaked shavings, and other trash. The investigator plucked the terrified hamsters out of the garbage.

She rushed all five hamsters to a veterinarian and eventually adopted them herself. They were the lucky ones, the survivors.

Many animals at Rainbow World Exotics didn't make it out alive.

At the facility, we captured horrifying footage showing that a worker castrated poorly anesthetized rabbits with a dull razor and wiped their open incisions with Clorox Disinfecting Wipes. Rabbits kicked and struggled during the surgery.

One supervisor deliberately stepped on a loose hamster, then "squashed" the animal with his hand, and tossed him or her—likely still alive—into the trash.

A cockatoo apparently died of exposure in a room that had gotten too cold. Many animals were denied vital veterinary care, including ferrets with rectal prolapses, a guinea pig with a broken hip, hamsters with a nasty bacterial disease, and animals injured in fights with their deeply frustrated cage-mates.

One baby Goffin's cockatoo, named Angel by PETA's investigator, wasted away for weeks. She cried out in misery from her barren cage before she grew so weak that she didn't even have the strength to flap away the flies that buzzed around her eyes. Despite the investigator's pleas, Angel was never taken to a veterinarian. She died in her cramped, filthy cage.

By contrast, Trey, Lily, Rusty, Colt, and Meeka began to thrive and display their true personalities after being rescued by PETA's investigator.

Meeka and Lily spent most of their days sleeping, cuddled up together, but at night, they loved to play and run in their wheels. Meeka was always the first to come out and say hello, while Lily hung back, a little shy.

The three boys loved to eat and were always excited about trying new foods. Rusty was an explorer who liked to dig and make underground trails. Trey and Colt stuffed their cheek pouches with snacks and followed Rusty through the paths.

All five hamsters blossomed into happy, healthy, cherished family members—five little reminders that all life has value. But far too many animals are still treated like disposable objects, not living, feeling beings, by the pet industry. Many of them won't live long enough to be given names by loving guardians. They'll never know a kind word or a gentle touch, and we'll never know their stories.

CHAPTER 9

BRANDI

Escape from an Unnatural Disaster

When BP's Deepwater Horizon oil-drilling rig exploded and pumped an estimated 210 million gallons of oil into the Gulf of Mexico, it wasn't just the worst oil spill in history, which was bad enough. Thousands of marine animals —from tiny zooplankton and crab larvae to dolphins, seabirds, and turtles—were poisoned and killed by the oozing muck that polluted 68,000 square miles of sea and 490 miles of beaches. The mammoth spill also completely shut down marine-associated industries for months, putting thousands of people out of work—and companion animals out of their homes.

Area animal shelters were inundated with a tidal wave of animals surrendered by people who had lost their jobs. Shelters that were already bursting at the seams were pushed to the breaking point. The local humane society sent out a distress call, and PETA answered. Thanks to the generosity of longtime PETA supporter Pamela Anderson, who paid for the animals' transportation and veterinary costs, PETA was able to evacuate more than 70 animals from shelters in the region. Pamela even flew to New Orleans to help care for the animals before their journey east. She became so smitten with two of the dogs that she adopted them on the spot.

45

Within days of the animals' arrival at PETA's headquarters in Norfolk, Virginia, nearly all of them had been placed in foster or permanent homes—except for Brandi, Bubbles, and Marshall.

These three cats had been removed from a depressing "no-kill" shelter, which, like so many of these facilities, was chronically severely crowded and filthy and often turned away vulnerable animals because it was full. It consisted of a patchwork cluster of cinder block and corrugated metal structures. The cats' cages were stacked on top of each other, and although the cats were let out of their cages from time to time, the floors were covered with urine, feces, hairballs, and trash. Litter pans, which went for days without being cleaned, overflowed with the cats' waste. The shelter wasn't air-conditioned, either, and cats panted in the bayou heat.

Imagine what it must have felt like to be ware-housed that way—confined to a cage, unable to take more than a step or two in any direction, the days stretching into months or years. If you cried to be let out, you were told to be quiet or were just ignored, your cries having become part of the background noise. There you sat, day after day, night after night, often forced to live amid your own waste.

Most "no-kill" facilities have attractive names and call themselves "rescues" and "sanctuaries." But many won't let anyone inside to see the poor conditions in which animals are kept. They reduce once joyful, energetic animals to hopeless, neurotic, pathetic shadows of their former selves. This is no life. Third-world prisons offer inmates more than this.

PETA purposely chose to evacuate "special needs" cats who seemed the least likely to be adopted. Many of the cats had respiratory infections, skin conditions, tumors, and abscesses, among other illnesses, as well as injuries. One cat had a misshapen face and rotten teeth. Another had a severe ulcer on her cornea, a wound on her back, and evidence of a long-term flea infestation.

Brandi, who had recently given birth to a litter of kittens, was nearly bald from stress and flea allergies. Marshall was missing most of a hind leg and half of his tail. Bubbles was neurotic and almost leaped out of her skin at every noise.

Weeks passed, and no one stepped forward to adopt the three misfits from PETA. While all of Brandi's kittens were adopted, her mangy appearance put people off. Bubbles would be lost without Marshall, and nobody wanted the package deal. Staffers who had gotten attached to the cats while they lived at the PETA office awaiting adoption suggested that they become PETA's official feline ambassadors, so the cats set up permanent residence at PETA's Virginia office, the Sam Simon Center.

Today, Brandi is barely recognizable—with a proper diet and a stress-free environment in which she is showered with affection all day long, her gorgeous tortoiseshell fur has grown back lush and silky. Bubbles, the "baby" of the trio, is a constant blur of activity, chasing catnip toys, scaling the backs of chairs, and making acrobatic leaps to catch paper balls. X-rays solved the mystery of Marshall's missing leg and tail—he still has buckshot lodged in his spine, telltale evidence of the cruel people he encountered during his harrowing life on the streets. But Marshall doesn't let his missing leg slow him down. He and Bubbles love to "drag race" up and down the halls— and sometimes he even wins.

CHAPTER 10

PETER AND JERRY
No Milk for These Babies

Peter and Jerry were born on a dairy farm in Pennsylvania. The cows on this farm weren't given names. Instead, they were identified by the numbers on the tags punched through their ears. The two male calves were discovered near death by a whistleblower who became a PETA investigator, and she was the one who gave them their names. She spent five months documenting the day-to-day operations on a massive factory farm that supplied milk to butter-manufacturing giant Land O'Lakes. What she saw was enough to make people want to spill their milk.

Cows sometimes stood knee-deep in mud and manure. Some cows suffering from respiratory illnesses had pus and mucus streaming down their faces. Abscesses were common on the farm—some of them burst and oozed pus, even while cows were being milked! Animals who were too sick or injured to stand were kicked, jabbed with electric prods, or stabbed with pocket knives in order to force them to struggle to their feet.

One cow suffering from a bacterial infection called "hoof rot" was forced to hobble around in agony after her hoof broke off. After another cow's gangrenous, infected teat ruptured, the suggested "treatment" was to wrap an elastic band around the teat in order to "amputate" it. The cow's condition deteriorated for 11 days before she finally died.

As on most dairy farms, calves on this farm were considered an unwanted "byproduct." The cows had to give birth in order to produce milk, but the milk was intended for humans, not calves, so the calves were torn away from their mothers shortly after birth. The males were useless—they couldn't be milked—so they were sent to slaughter, usually when they were just a few months old.

Many of the male calves on this farm were confined to filthy pens while they awaited slaughter. Jerry was found hobbling as best he could on deformed legs, after escaping from a holding pen. He was painfully thin, infested with lice, and nearly blind as a result of pinkeye, a painful bacterial infection that's common in the filthy conditions typical of factory farms. Many calves on the farm went blind from pinkeye.

Peter was found two months later, lying in a filthy pen, too weak and sick to stand or even lift his head. He was caked from head to toe with the manure and urine in which he and other calves were forced to live. After PETA's investigator gained custody of Peter, she rushed him to a veterinarian who determined that he was suffering from pneumonia, dehydration, ringworm, pinkeye, and lice. Peter was so malnourished that the vet estimated he was nearly 100 pounds underweight. PETA's investigator bought both calves and whisked them away to a "safe house" until they could be driven to their new home at a sanctuary.

Although he arrived at the sanctuary more than two months after Jerry did, Peter instantly bonded with the other calf and cried mournfully whenever Jerry left his side, even for a moment. Jerry, in turn, looked around for Peter if the younger calf didn't immediately follow. But as the calves grew, their roles reversed. Jerry's eyesight was permanently impaired by pinkeye scarring, so Peter acted as a kind of "seeing-eye cow." But eventually, Jerry's health began to deteriorate, and after several years of bucolic bliss, reveling in chin scratches, eating apple treats, and hanging out with his best friends, Peter and Patrick the pig, he was euthanized. He left this world as quietly as he lived in it, but the steer with the gentle spirit left a permanent mark on the hearts of all those who knew him.

CHAPTER 11

MADELINE

The Chicken Who Was Left Behind

If you take a drive through the countryside, you will likely pass several chicken farms—although you might not realize that's what you're looking at. The typical chicken factory farm is composed of several long, low-slung, windowless metal sheds. At first glance, you might assume they're warehouses of some kind that are used to store farm equipment or hay. Surely they don't keep living beings in such places?

Oh, but they do.

Madeline was one of those living beings. Two PETA fieldworkers were on their way to a call in rural North Carolina when they spotted a flash of white in the field next to an empty Perdue chicken barn. Was it a stray plastic bag or a discarded Styrofoam container? It went by in a flash as they drove down the highway, but they could have sworn it was a chicken.

The fieldworkers turned around and returned to the farm, pulling their van into the driveway. There she was, a very small chicken, wandering all alone in the field, just a few feet away from speeding cars. Madeline was only a few weeks old, still a baby, just like all "broiler" chickens when they are sent to slaughter. The average age of slaughtered "broilers" is just 6 or 7 weeks, younger than a weaned kitten. They are killed before they ever get a chance to live.

She likely had been left behind when the rest of the birds in the barn were rounded up for the trip to the slaughterhouse. Perhaps Madeline had fled the scary people who grabbed the other chickens by the wings, legs, or neck and slammed them into transport cages as they shrieked in terror and pain. Maybe she had simply been overlooked in the confusion or had been purposely left behind because she was under-sized.

Madeline may have seemed like the luckiest chicken in the world, but her reprieve was only temporary. There was no way she was going to survive by herself: She had no food or water, she couldn't fly, and her white feathers stood out like a beacon, making her extremely vulnerable to predators. She was all alone. Forgotten. Discarded like a piece of trash along the highway.

There was a man standing next to the barn, smoking a cigarette, seemingly oblivious to the little bird walking nearby. The fieldworkers approached him and asked if they could take the chicken, knowing that the man was unlikely to make any effort to care for her. Farmers accept some "losses" as the cost of doing business. When you cram tens of thousands of birds into a single shed and force them to live amid their own waste and inhale ammonia fumes from their own urine, some chickens inevitably get sick, as diseases spread like wildfire in such horrendous conditions. Or the birds' legs become crippled when their genetically manipulated bodies grow too fast, and they starve or die of dehydration when they can't reach food or water troughs. Or they die of heat exhaustion when the electricity goes out and the big fans grind to a halt.

This was just one little bird out of the thousands the farmer had just shipped out. A cog in the machine. The man shrugged his shoulders with infinite boredom. Whatever you want to do, crazy ladies.

The fieldworkers gently scooped Madeline up and put her in one of the cat carriers that they always have in the van. Perhaps she realized that she was safe, because she started gently cooing and murmuring to herself. Chickens have at least 24 different cries, chirps, and squawks to warn other birds about a predator, announce when they have laid an egg, or just say "good morning." Madeline kept up a constant stream of chatter all the way back to PETA's headquarters.

She spent the night there, charming everyone she met with her curiosity and friendliness, surprising in a bird who had been through what she had and had every reason to fear and flee from humans.

The next day, two staffers drove Madeline to a sanctuary, where she was placed in the infirmary for a few days to give her a chance to recover before she was transferred to a spacious barn and pasture, where the other rescued chickens lived.

It didn't take the intrepid little hen long to settle in at her new home. Chickens are extremely social animals, and Madeline quickly befriended the other birds—and the humans, too. She was once a small, forlorn bundle of dirty feathers, but she blossomed after she was rescued.

Madeline's rescuers can't fathom how people can justify killing and eating such smart, social, personable birds. The average American is responsible for the deaths of approximately 2,500 chickens over his or her lifetime—billions of chickens are slaughtered for food in the U.S. alone every year. When you consider the sheer volume—the number of lives involved and the enormous suffering that each bird endures—chickens may well be the most abused animals on the planet.

Chickens aren't vegetables or walking entrées—they are living, feeling individuals who have distinct personalities and interests. Just ask Madeline—she'll tell you.

The greatness of a nation and its moral progress can be judged by the way its animals are treated.

—Mohandas K. Gandhi

CHAPTER 12

SUNDER

Seven Years a Slave

In India, elephants are revered for their link to the elephant-headed Hindu god Ganesh. But this doesn't mean that elephants are treated like deities. Far from it. Rather, their religious ties can cause them to be terribly abused—chained up at temples and used as living good luck charms, props for religious ceremonies, and tourist attractions.

Such was the plight of a young elephant named Sunder. We don't know the ugly details of Sunder's capture, but we do know that he was only 7 years old—still a baby—when he was torn away from his mother and donated by a rich and powerful politician to an Indian temple, where he spent the next six years restrained by all four legs with chains and spiked tethers, being beaten over and over again. Lonely and in constant fear of his next beating, Sunder spent day after day unable to take so much as a single step in any direction. The chains ate into his skin, resulting in oozing, infected wounds. He never saw his mother or his family again.

PETA India fought long and hard to free Sunder. More than 220,000 people around the world wrote to authorities seeking Sunder's release, and many celebrities—including Paul McCartney, Pamela Anderson, the late Sam Simon, and Bollywood superstars Amitabh Bachchan, Madhuri Dixit, Gulshan Grover, Celina Jaitly, and Arjun Rampal—took to Twitter or wrote letters to keep the spotlight on Sunder's plight.

But Sunder's owner stubbornly refused to listen. Even after Indian officials ordered him to free Sunder, he flouted the law, took the elephant away from the temple, and attempted to hide him in a chicken shed, where he languished for another year.

Undaunted, PETA India pleaded Sunder's case in court in a battle that climbed all the way to India's Supreme Court. The judges ruled in PETA India's favor, ordering that the elephant be moved to the spacious Bannerghatta Biological Park in Bangalore.

Within a week of the verdict, Sunder was being readied for transport. Staffers with PETA India and the PETA-supported charity Animal Rahat ("Rahat" means "Relief" in Hindi) braved near rioting by the politician's supporters when loading Sunder onto a transport truck. Despite a police escort, staffers at times feared for their and Sunder's safety as men on motorcycles harassed them on the first leg of the journey. But Sunder remained calm, and everyone arrived safely.

Once at the sanctuary, Sunder was finally able to socialize with other elephants for the first time since he was a baby. Because he had spent so much time in isolation, nobody was quite sure how he would react. But he was instantly smitten by a beautiful female elephant named Lakshmi, and he quickly befriended a male elephant named Van Raj. Sunder was also fascinated by the park's youngest resident, baby Shiva, gently touching her with his trunk.

Sunder arrived at the sanctuary with a severe leg injury caused by long-term chaining, which required close monitoring for several weeks. But as soon as his leg healed, he was allowed free run of the park's 122 acres of forests, streams, and ponds. When Sunder went for his first swim, he splashed excitedly and "snorkeled" using his trunk.

It took some time for Sunder to realize that there would be no more beatings, that he could trust his new caretakers. But everyone worked hard to earn his trust—giving him tasty coconuts and other treats was part of that process—and Sunder quickly made progress. Fresh air, sunshine, a tranquil lake, and dappled forests are now his to enjoy with his friends every day, but it's unlikely that he will ever take them for granted.

CHAPTER 13

J.R. and Terry

Life after Solitary Confinement

His life in the lush African jungle must have seemed like a distant dream to J.R. It had been over two decades since the 26-year-old chimpanzee had been torn away from his family and home, when he was just a youngster.

One day, he was likely roughhousing with his siblings and cousins, getting into mischief and being reprimanded by his watchful mother. The next thing he knew, he was in a cage, terrified and confused. His mother, father, sisters, and brothers were all gone. There was no one to turn to for comfort. No one's hand to hold. Just fear, loneliness, and despair.

At best, J.R. may have spent hours in the noisy hold of a transport plane. Worse, he might have spent days or weeks in a crate in the bowels of a ship.

There was no relief when the trip ended. J.R. found himself halfway around the world, in a strange and frightening place where people yelled at him and hit him with sticks that stung like wasps in order to force him to perform confusing and uncomfortable tricks. Why were they angry at him? Why wasn't his mother there to protect him? The circus must have seemed like a totally alien world to J.R., as if he had landed on another planet.

After a few years in the circus, J.R. had grown too big and strong to be handled safely. Like other performing chimpanzees, he had "aged out" and needed to be warehoused somewhere for the rest of his life, which could be several decades. So J.R. was sent to a notoriously substandard North Carolina roadside zoo that was the subject of multiple PETA complaints before its federal license was ultimately revoked. J.R. spent the next decade there all alone in a small cage.

Chimpanzees are social animals who need the company and companionship of others. Like humans, they love, laugh, play, and grieve. But J.R. had no one.

As if a decade in solitary confinement weren't punishment enough, J.R. was then transferred to another seedy zoo that was also the subject of multiple PETA complaints. Confined alone to a cage no larger than a typical garage, J.R. wandered in aimless circles, screamed in frustration, flung his body against the wire fence, and repeatedly bit his own arms, a heartbreaking symptom of captivity-induced psychosis.

Would J.R. know a moment of happiness ever again? Yes, he would, thanks to a generous PETA Investigations & Rescue Fund supporter who paid all the costs associated with J.R.'s transfer to the spacious, tropical Save the Chimps sanctuary in Florida. After 20 years in hell, J.R. had finally arrived in paradise.

Instead of a world measured in a few square feet, J.R. now has acres of lush green grass to walk on, palm trees to relax under, "jungle gyms" to climb on, balmy weather to bask in, and natural, wholesome foods to eat.

J.R. is no longer alone. He has a group of other

rescued chimpanzees to socialize with, including Indie, his new best friend.

Just a few months after J.R. got to the sanctuary, another chimpanzee arrived with a similar history.

Like J.R., Terry had spent nearly two decades alone. For years, PETA had tried desperately to persuade the owner of the decrepit Las Vegas Zoo, where Terry was caged, to send the chimpanzee to a sanctuary. But he refused, and one interminable year turned into the next.

As a testament to just how dire things were at this facility, one day all the zookeepers simply quit. Walked out. The zoo's doors closed for good shortly afterward. Finally, Terry had a chance at a real life.

The moment PETA heard about the zoo's closure, we contacted the North American Primate Sanctuary Alliance to appeal for Terry's transfer to a sanctuary instead of to another roadside zoo. That required funds, and that same generous Investigations & Rescue Fund supporter stepped up to the plate again, along with another wonderful PETA President's Circle patron. With their generous support, PETA was able to contribute to Terry's transfer to Save the Chimps.

Terry is a handsome guy. While he's curious and interested in what's going on around him, he's understandably a bit shy. His caretakers say that he has a special fondness for oranges, bouncy balls, and, of all things, piñatas.

J.R. and Terry have gone from having nothing to having everything that means anything to a chimpanzee.

CHAPTER 14

BELLA AND EDWARD

A Hollywood Ending for Bella and Edward

For five long years, Bella and Edward's whole world consisted of a cramped cage inside the "mammal room" at U.S. Global Exotics' (USGE) massive warehouse in Arlington, Texas. During that time, the two ring-tailed lemurs had nothing but each other—no toys, no blankets, no trees to climb on, no room to explore, nowhere to hide.

In their native Madagascar, these intelligent, social primates would be swinging through treetops, scampering over rocks, munching on tamarinds, and relaxing in the sun, but at USGE's dismal warehouse, they never left their cramped cage for so much as a second. Like concentration camp prisoners, they lived in a state of constant fear of their captors and huddled in a corner of their cage, clinging to each other, whenever anyone approached.

Bella and Edward didn't initially have names. The devoted pair was named after the *Twilight* saga's star-crossed lovers by PETA's investigator, who spent seven months documenting almost unimaginable horrors at USGE—at the time, one of the nation's largest exotic-animal dealers.

USGE bought and sold wild-caught and captive-bred animals all over the world, including to companies that supplied Petco and PetSmart. Small animals were subjected to appalling conditions and chronic neglect, sometimes being kept for days or weeks in pillowcases, shipping boxes, or even 2-liter soda bottles with no food or water.

The neglect is hardly surprising when you consider that USGE kept *tens of thousands* of hamsters, gerbils, hedgehogs, chinchillas, ferrets, snakes, lizards, turtles, frogs, wallabies, sloths, anteaters, kinkajous, and other exotic animals at its facility yet employed a staff of *just three or four people* to care for them.

Bella and Edward and other mammals were locked inside barren cages, bins, and metal troughs, sometimes for months or, in the lemurs' case, even years. Some of the animals went insane from the intensive confinement, pacing, circling, and performing incessant backflips in their cages. Some clawed frantically at the cage bars in a futile attempt to escape. Others became depressed and refused to eat.

USGE's owners routinely ordered that sick and injured animals—including a squirrel whose neck had been so badly wounded that the muscle was exposed and a chinchilla who was bleeding from a prolapsed rectum—be frozen to death. Hundreds of squirrels, lizards, and snakes were killed in USGE's freezer, in which some animals remained alive for hours before finally dying.

Bella and Edward were very sensitive to the suffering of other animals. On one occasion, an injured squirrel in the same room was making distress calls as he died. Soon after, one of the lemurs began to cry

68

out mournfully and repeatedly.

Over the years, Bella and Edward had at least three babies, all of whom were taken away from them within days of birth and sold. The lemurs were inconsolable, screaming and crying for weeks every time one of their babies was stolen.

PETA took the evidence gathered by our investigator to the U.S. Fish & Wildlife Service, and soon afterward, local authorities, working with PETA, confiscated more than 26,000 animals, the largest animal seizure in history. USGE shut its doors for good, a federal arrest warrant was issued for the former owner (who had fled the country), and the facility's attending veterinarian was fined $2,500.

Bella and Edward were moved to a temporary holding facility with trees, toys, blankets, and a floor that was covered with aspen bedding instead of the wire bars of a cage. It was the first time in at least five years that their feet had touched solid ground. Their new diet included a variety of fruits and vegetables, including bananas (their favorite!), grapes, mangoes, sweet potatoes, and kiwis. Soon, they were climbing the trees, chewing on branches, running around, and playing.

A few weeks later, Bella and Edward were transferred to a permanent home at the Detroit Zoo, a progressive zoo that offers rehabilitation and sanctuary to captive exotic animals rescued from circuses, roadside zoos, and other facilities. There, Bella and Edward finally have the chance to live as lemurs again—instead of as "merchandise."

69

CHAPTER 15

ANNA AND GREG

Ailing Pregnant Donkey Finds Room at the Inn

When rescuers first saw Anna, her belly was hugely swollen with a foal who seemed ready to arrive at any minute. Like many donkeys in India, Anna was forced to work at the brick kilns, toiling under the merciless sun hauling heavy loads of bricks for up to 14 hours a day.

Even when the temperatures soared to 140 degrees Fahrenheit, as they often do in the summer in India, Anna got no relief. Most of the time she wasn't even afforded a sip of water to cool her dry, burning mouth, because, like many drivers, her owner mistakenly believed that the water would slow her down.

He piled as many as 50 bricks at a time onto her back and forced her to haul the heavy loads without so much as a blanket to protect her sensitive skin from the bricks' sharp edges. Her light-gray coat bore telltale scars from the bloody wounds that the bricks had cut into her skin. Some of her scars were also likely from beatings that she had received to force her to keep working when the dehydration, muscle strain, and exhaustion started to take their toll. She was also suffering from a painful skin condition, making it impossible for her to enjoy rolling on the ground to scratch her back at the end of a long day, as donkeys love to do.

After she gave birth, Anna would likely have been sent right back to work, where she would have had to see her baby sentenced to work in the brick kilns right alongside her. The foal might have had his nostrils slashed with a knife, as many owners believe that doing so will allow the donkeys to breathe more deeply and thus work harder. He probably would have been denied sufficient food, water, and veterinary care, and he would also likely have been beaten. If he had broken a leg or sustained another catastrophic injury, it is likely that he would have been abandoned and left to die.

But Animal Rahat had other plans.

This PETA-supported organization was founded to improve the lives of India's working animals. The Animal Rahat team provides free or low-cost veterinary services, educates animals' owners about basic care, and guides them away from cruel practices. The organization also maintains treatment and retirement centers where sick animals can be rehabilitated and those who are too old or disabled to continue working can live out their remaining years in peace instead of being abandoned or sent to slaughter.

Just a week after Animal Rahat rescued Anna, she gave birth. The staff members named her sweet newborn Greg. They delighted in watching the well-fed and well-rested new mother dote on her foal and in knowing that she would never have to watch her precious baby suffer through long, hard days at the brick kilns.

Today, Anna and Greg spend peaceful days together ambling around the fields of Animal Rahat's retirement home. Greg gleefully darts about, scampering and playing with the other youngsters while his mother looks on from the shade of an old tree. Anna rests all she needs to, grazes as much as she likes, and lovingly nuzzles her baby whenever she wants to. Instead of seeing nothing but hard-packed roads and brick kilns, Anna and Greg now gaze out over the beautiful Nilgiri hills, the perfect backdrop for their beautiful new life.

CHAPTER 16

GEORGIA BEAR PITS

This Place Is the Pits

In the darkest days of the Vietnam War, prisoners were dumped in dungeon-like pits where they spent their days looking up in desperation for a ray of sunshine or a breath of fresh air. Unable to see, smell, or hear nearly anything beyond the four walls, the captives sometimes went mad from sensory deprivation.

Such conditions are eerily similar to those endured by 17 bears at the Black Forest Bear Park in Georgia. These animals weren't prisoners of war, but they were prisoners nonetheless.

Day after day, year after year, the bears saw nothing but concrete walls and floors. Some bears just shut down altogether and would sit and stare at a blank wall like a patient in an insane asylum. Others paced from one side of the pit to the other for hours on end without let-up. The only break in their monotonous existence was stopping to beg visitors to toss food down to them from the walkway above.

When the bears simply could not stomach one more stale piece of bread or withered chunk of apple, the uneaten food would rot on the ground, a putrid stew of food, feces, and urine.

When it rained, the bears got soaked. When the Georgia heat and humidity skyrocketed, they sweltered. Some of the pits had small pools, but they were often allowed to dry up.

The female bears were bred repeatedly, only to have their cubs taken away shortly after they were born. The cubs were placed in glass boxes about the size of a telephone booth so that visitors could get up close to them, gawking, giggling, and tapping on the glass. Everyone knows how protective mama bears are, yet they were helpless to protect their vulnerable babies. One bear, O.B., was so traumatized by the kidnappings that she had to be tied up.

After PETA told *The Simpsons* co-creator Sam Simon about the bears' plight, he quickly came to the rescue. In conjunction with the Atlanta Humane Society and PETA patron and Atlanta Humane Society Executive Committee Vice Chair Anna J. Ware, we worked quickly to get the bears out of the pits and moved to The Wild Animal Sanctuary in Colorado. Shortly afterward, the miserable roadside zoo shut its doors forever.

Every detail of the bears' trip was carefully planned, including making arrangements for "emergency contingency locations" along the route —on-call facilities available if any health-related emergency were to arise. Luckily, no such stops were needed, and the bears seemed comfortable on the ride, snacking on tasty treats all along the way.

The bears' emotions as they took their first steps out of the truck ranged from tentative to ecstatic. Some bears, such as Dakota, charged out like they owned the place and never looked back.

One-year-old cubs Howell and Mansell were so thrilled with their new home that they were almost delirious with glee, climbing on everything in sight.

Others, perhaps thinking it was all too good to be true, took their time getting used to feeling grass beneath their feet for the first time in their lives.

A few weeks after they arrived, O.B. and another bear, Ursula, who were both pregnant at the time of the move, each gave birth to three cubs in cozy, private dens.

No one came to take the little ones away. No one is going to. For the first time, Ursula and O.B. won't have to live in fear of having their babies kidnapped. They can raise and nurture and love them in peace.

These six little ones will never know the misery of a jail cell. They'll frolic and play and grow up with others of their own kind, surrounded by lush vegetation. When they want to cool off—or goof off —all they have to do is jump into the nearest pond.

CHAPTER 17

NOLA

Rescuing a Hurricane's Forgotten Victims

When rescuers found her, the young Pomeranian was all by herself, trembling in the middle of a flooded New Orleans highway. A temporary plastic collar with the name of the highway scrawled with a permanent marker hung around her thin neck.

Nola was one of an estimated 250,000 animals who were separated from their families in 2005 because of Hurricane Katrina, a major hurricane that destroyed levees and submerged entire neighborhoods.

Nola was one of the lucky ones who survived.

When natural disasters strike around the globe, rescuers from PETA and our international affiliates often travel straight into the hardest-hit areas to rescue animals who have been displaced, abandoned, or lost. PETA's emergency animal rescue team arrived in New Orleans seven days after Hurricane Katrina hit, when animal rescuers—who had been delayed by red tape, the emergency evacuation, and threats of violence—were at last allowed access to the submerged city.

Time was not on their side.

Thousands of animals had been left behind in

situations from which they couldn't escape, trapped inside cages, chained to trees, or locked up behind closed doors as the waters rushed in. Other terrified animals were clinging to trees, swimming madly in the flooded streets, or pacing, stranded, and left to die on rooftops and balconies. They desperately needed rescuing, and many anguished people who had been forced to leave them behind or had been elsewhere when the levees burst were prevented from returning to help them.

PETA's team knocked down doors, crawled through filth, broke through padlocked fences, and waded through toxic floodwaters to rescue animals who, in many cases, were barely clinging to life. The work was grueling, with dawn-to-midnight workdays in temperatures that sometimes exceeded 100 degrees Fahrenheit and nights spent sleeping fitfully in sweltering vans swarming with insects. The team's rescue missions grew increasingly urgent with each passing day as animals who had survived the floods began to succumb to starvation, dehydration, and heat exhaustion.

The team's most heartbreaking missions were the ones that came too late.

One helpless dog who had been locked inside a bathroom had survived for three weeks until the team arrived, only to die in the arms of her rescuer. Another dog, one of countless pit bulls the team found who had obviously been bred for fighting, had died in a carrier after desperately chewing a hole in it that wasn't quite large enough for her to fit through.

Other animals were saved after miraculously surviving for weeks in hellish conditions.

One dog who had been tied to a staircase railing had been forced to tread floodwaters as they rose around him, judging from the high water mark on the wall.

Another dog, who the rescuers later discovered was deaf, must have felt the vibrations as the team battered down the front door. She was heard frantically scratching and pawing at the door of the closet she had been put in. As soon as the door was opened, she burst out of the closet and covered her rescuers' faces with kisses of gratitude.

With the help of sympathetic federal, state, and local officials, PETA's team rescued more than 300 dogs, cats, birds, and other animals. PETA also helped feed, water, walk, and care for thousands more at what became the world's largest emergency animal shelter, at the Lamar-Dixon Expo Center in Gonzales, Louisiana.

Nola was one of the 32 dogs rescued by the PETA team and evacuated to our headquarters, the Sam Simon Center, in Norfolk, Virginia. Staffers and volunteers fostered the dogs while we searched for their guardians.

At first, Nola's foster mom (who became her permanent mom when her guardian couldn't be found) harbored the mistaken belief that she was a surprisingly quiet little Pomeranian. Little did she know that Nola's true personality had been frightened out of her—but only temporarily.

After a month of TLC and overcoming a nasty case of kennel cough, the real Nola emerged—the one who could outswim any big dog, loved to chase the beam of a flashlight across the yard, and was always quick with a kiss or a cuddle.

Never doubt that a small group of thoughtful, committed citizens can change the world.

—Margaret Mead

CHAPTER 18

FELIX AND BRONSON

A Kitten's Worst Nightmare

To look at brothers Felix and Bronson now as they race around their home roughhousing and making death-defying leaps off the backs of chairs, it's hard to picture them as sickly newborn kittens clinging to life. But that's exactly what they were when a PETA investigator discovered them at Caboodle Ranch, Inc., during a five-month undercover investigation at the "no-kill" hoarding facility masquerading as a "sanctuary."

Caboodle Ranch billed itself to the public as a "cat rescue sanctuary" that promised to give cats "everything they will ever need to live a happy healthy life." But what PETA uncovered belied the idyllic image presented on Caboodle's website. Cats were confined to filthy, dilapidated trailers and sheds and were forced to live amid their own vomit and waste. Maggots covered cats' food bowls as well as the medications that were kept in a moldy refrigerator.

Cats suffered from open wounds, parasites, corneal ulcers, and upper respiratory infections so severe that they gasped for air and struggled to breathe. Animals with green mucus dripping from their eyes and noses wandered around, spreading disease to other cats. Some cats died after suffering for weeks without veterinary care.

One such cat was Lilly, whose iris protruded through a ruptured cornea and who suffered for months despite attempts by PETA's investigator to help. The investigator offered to take Lilly to a veterinarian or even to adopt the cat, but Caboodle's founder and operator, Craig Grant, refused to allow it. Lilly eventually died after months of neglect.

Kittens, who should have been full of spunk and high spirits, often became sick and listless at Caboodle. PETA's investigator found one little white kitten all alone, with eyes so encrusted with dried discharge that they couldn't open. She pointed out the obvious illness to Grant, but instead of providing the kitten with veterinary care, he simply told the investigator to put the kitten with a cat who had given birth to three other kittens—Felix, Bronson, and Luna. Within a month, the little white kitten had died, apparently of an untreated upper respiratory infection.

Desperate to save the other three kittens, the investigator begged Grant to give them to her, and she rushed them to a veterinary hospital. There, they were treated for upper respiratory infections and dehydration. But just two days later, little Luna was struggling to breathe, so the investigator rushed her to an emergency animal hospital. As a result of the neglect that Luna had endured at Caboodle, she was now battling anemia, hypoglycemia, and hypothermia. Despite shots of dextrose to raise her blood sugar and a heating pad to stave off the hypothermia,

Luna was too weak to fight, and at a veterinarian's recommendation, she was euthanized to avoid prolonging her suffering.

Felix and Bronson faced a tough battle, too, but after months of intensive care by PETA's investigator, both kittens recovered and were placed in a new home, where they quickly made fast friends with the resident dog and parrot.

Officials in Madison County, Florida, used the evidence gathered by PETA to raid Caboodle Ranch and, with the aid of other humane organizations, seized nearly 700 cats from Caboodle's property, moldy trailers, and ammonia-ridden sheds. They arrested Grant on cruelty-to-animals and other charges, including two felonies. Like Felix and Bronson, the other surviving cats finally received the care and affection that they had long been denied.

CHAPTER 19

ACTIVISM IDEAS

Changing Minds, Saving Lives

U nlike the animals you have read about in this book, many animals abused in the food, fur, experimentation, entertainment, and pet industries will not have happy endings. We can help prevent future abuse by working with major corporations, policymakers, prosecutors, and sheriff's offices and by showing people what happens to animals inside factory farms, fur farms, laboratories, circuses, and zoos so that they can make informed, compassionate choices.

No one who believes that kindness is a virtue can argue that it's acceptable to be cruel when we have the option to be kind—when we can eat tasty vegan foods instead of animal flesh or support cruelty-free companies instead of those that drip shampoo into rabbits' eyes.

By supporting PETA's Investigations & Rescue Fund, you'll be helping PETA's investigators expose— and ultimately stop—cruelty to animals used for food, clothing, experimentation, and entertainment. You'll also be making it possible for PETA to provide animals with veterinary treatment, transport, and shelter in emergencies. But there are many other ways that you can help animals every day, just by making kind choices when you go about your daily routine.

Here are some simple things that you can do—and encourage others to do—to help reduce animal suffering, protect the environment, and promote healthy living:

Try Vegan

- Order one of PETA's free vegan starter kits at PETA.org/VSK. The kit is packed with recipes, shopping tips, nutrition information, and more. Get a stack to drop off at local businesses.

- Opt for great-tasting dairy-free milks, vegan margarines, and egg replacers when making cakes and other baked goods.

- Take nonperishable vegan food items such as oatmeal, rice, beans, and aseptic boxes of soy milk to your local food bank.

- Ask your local schools to offer vegan options in the cafeteria. Visit peta2.com for a packet of helpful resources.

- Make vegan meals for potlucks, office parties, and other functions. Most people won't even notice if you substitute mock meats, soy milk, and other tasty vegan foods for animal-based ones in popular recipes. But be sure to share the recipe—there are hundreds of delicious vegan recipes at PETA.org—and let everyone know that each vegan saves more than 100 animals every year.

- Talk to managers of restaurants with lobster tanks about the cruelty of capturing and boiling live crustaceans and ask them to stop serving lobster.

Shed Your Skins

- Instead of buying bags, belts, or shoes made from the skins of snakes, lizards, alligators, cows, goats, or pigs, shop for cruelty-free fashions using PETA's "Shopping Guide to Compassionate Clothing," available at PETA.org.

- If you don't see a selection of nonleather shoes, handbags, and belts in local stores, approach the managers and politely ask them to carry vegan items.

- Complain whenever you see that fur is being sold. Be sure to tell the manager that you will never shop there again as long as the store sells fur.

- Are old, unwanted furs cluttering up your closet? Send them to PETA to be given to homeless people and wildlife rehabilitators or to be used in educational events.

- Share the disturbing footage from PETA's wool investigation (available at PETA.org) and encourage others to choose humane fabrics, such as cotton, polyester, nylon, and rayon.

Be a Caring Consumer

- Choose cruelty-free cosmetics, toiletries, and cleaning supplies. More than 1,000 companies have pledged not to test their products on animals. Many companies, including Citra Solv, Earth Friendly Products, Ecover, and Method Products, Inc., make household products that are both eco- and animal-friendly. Visit PETA.org for lists of companies that do and that don't test on animals.

- Donate only to health charities that don't fund experiments on animals. Find a list of humane charities at PETA.org/HumaneSeal.

- Contact companies that conduct cruel experiments on animals, including Procter & Gamble, Clorox, Unilever, Colgate-Palmolive Co., and S.C. Johnson, and tell them that you won't buy their products until they go cruelty-free for good.

Enjoy Animal-Free Activities

- Patronize only animal-free circuses, such as Cirque du Soleil and The FSU Flying High Circus. These circuses are not only animal-friendly but also truly awe-inspiring. Learn more about circus cruelty at RinglingBeatsAnimals.com.

- Avoid cruel events such as greased-pig contests, donkey basketball games, and horse and dog races.

Call the sponsors of upcoming events that use animals and explain why they shouldn't sponsor animal exhibits. Post comments on the sponsor's Facebook page, too, and ask everyone you know to do the same.

- Urge everyone you know—and even those you don't know—to stay away from SeaWorld and other marine *abuse*ment parks. Find out more at SeaWorldOfHurt.com.

- Stay away from all zoos—even the accredited ones often breed animals and sell the "surplus" ones to canned-hunting ranches. And teach children why zoos can't meet the needs of highly social and intelligent animals. Visit PETA.org to find out more.

- Ask your child's teacher to stop keeping animals in the classroom or requiring students to dissect animals. Visit TeachKind.org for information on non-animal teaching methods and humane-education tips.

Live in Harmony with Wildlife

- If you encounter a baby animal, his or her mom and dad will typically be nearby keeping a watchful eye. It's usually best not to intervene unless the animal is injured or sick. Call your local humane society for a list of licensed wildlife rehabilitators who can offer advice.

- Always take along reusable cloth bags when shopping in order to help save forests and marine animals, who often mistake plastic bags floating in the ocean for food and eat them.

- Shoot wildlife with a camera instead of with a gun or bow and arrow. Hiking, camping, and canoeing are just a few of the many ways to enjoy the outdoors without harming animals.

- Attract birds, butterflies, and other wildlife to your yard by planting shrubs and flowers and adding nesting boxes, seasonal feeders, and a fresh water source.

- Choose organic, shade-grown, bird-friendly coffee beans—you'll be supporting companies that both pay workers fair wages and help preserve tropical forests for birds.

- Be nice to mice and rats. Instead of using cruel poisons or snap or glue traps, use a humane trap (available at PETACatalog.com) to live-trap rodents and release them into a wooded area. Prevent more animals from entering your home by sealing all holes. Store food in sealed containers, and keep floors and countertops clean. If your apartment or office building is using glue traps, ask the building manager to use humane options instead.

Be an Animal's Best Friend

- If you have room in your heart and home, adopt an animal from a shelter instead of buying one from a breeder or pet store. *Just remember*: Animals need a lifetime commitment. Make sure you will have the time and patience to exercise and play with your animal companion as well as the financial resources to pay for food, accessories, and veterinary care.

- Always spay or neuter cats and dogs, and urge your friends and neighbors to do the same. Offer to make the appointment, provide transportation, or even help pay for the surgery.

- Volunteer to walk dogs, clean cat cages, and play with animals at a nearby animal shelter. You can also help shelters by donating blankets, towels, toys, kitty litter, food, and other supplies.

- Offer to walk neighbors' dogs who are always tied up outdoors or left alone throughout the day. Make sure "backyard dogs" have food, fresh water, and shelter. If they don't, report it to the authorities.

- Take immediate action if you see an animal left alone in a vehicle. On a 78-degree day, the temperature inside a parked car can soar to between 100 and 120 degrees in just minutes. Call 911, and have the owner paged in the nearest buildings. Don't leave until the animal has been rescued.

- Call people who place "free to a good home" ads in papers or online to warn them that their animal might end up in the hands of a dogfighter, an experimenter, or another cruel person. Visit PETA.org for more information.

- Brake for animals, and keep an emergency rescue kit—including a carrier, a leash, a towel, treats, wet and dry cat food, and phone numbers of local animal control agencies, emergency veterinary hospitals, and wildlife rehabilitators—in your car to help stray or injured animals when traveling.

Other Ways to Get Active for Animals

- Wear T-shirts and buttons with animal rights messages, or put an animal rights bumper sticker or personalized license plate with a message such as "BAN FUR" on your car.

- Hang up one of PETA's "Rescued" calendars or keep a coffee mug with an animal rights message on your desk—they're great conversation starters.

- Set up an information table at a street fair or another community event—anywhere that there are people to talk to about animal rights. We can send you everything that you'll need and give you tons of great tips and talking points.

- Place animal rights literature in your local Laundromat, library, retirement home, or recreation center.

- Demonstrate! If there's a fur store in town or the circus is coming soon, why not organize a protest? PETA's Action Team will send you supplies and help promote the event.

- Raise funds to help animals by holding a yard sale, a vegan bake sale, or a car wash, or organize a bowl-a-thon, dance-a-thon, bike-a-thon, or any other "a-thon."

- Download PETA's iPhone/Android app to get action alerts delivered straight to your phone.

- Write letters about animal issues to the editor of your local newspaper or favorite magazines.

- Contact the producer of any TV program in which characters abuse or ridicule animals, and send an e-mail to the network that airs the show as well. Also, consider leaving negative comments on the network's Facebook pages.

- Make a personalized e-mail autosignature or record an animal rights message on your voice-mail or answering machine, such as "Each vegan saves more than 100 animals every year. For tips on how to go vegan, visit PETA.org."

- Ask local radio stations to run one of PETA's 30- or 60-second public service announcements.

- Share PETA information on social media. Keep up to date by "liking" PETA on Facebook and following us on Twitter.

Be an Advocate for Animals

As Elie Wiesel, chair of the President's Commission on the Holocaust, said in his 1986 Nobel Peace Prize acceptance speech, "Neutrality helps the oppressor, never the victim." Always speak up when you see or hear about animal abuse. Alert PETA or the appropriate authorities if you witness cruelty to or the neglect of an animal on a factory farm, in a laboratory, in a circus or zoo, in a pet store, or anywhere else.

YOU Can Make a Difference

It doesn't matter who you are or where you live—you can do something to help animals. Whatever we say, do, or buy makes a statement. Change can happen with the simplest of efforts. What you choose to do can be as ambitious as starting your own animal rights group or interning at PETA or as simple as supporting cruelty-free companies and eating vegan meals.

Our treatment of animals is a reflection of how we treat each other. When we treat animals with respect—and urge others to do the same—we help break the chains of violence and abuse and help create a better world for all the Earth's inhabitants.

Please read my book *The PETA Practical Guide to Animal Rights*, available at PETACatalog.com, for even more inspirational ideas.

Epilogue

It happens behind locked laboratory doors, in desolate cages that the public never sees. It happens in cold and lonely backyards hidden from the street. Often, the worst abuse and neglect of animals are hidden.

You may have thought as you read the stories in this book, "Why didn't more people do something?" As the animals' cries filled the air, how could caring individuals look away?

I am asking you right now—please don't look away. For every animal PETA rescues through our investigations, thousands more remain behind those closed doors, in those faraway places, or perhaps just around the corner—all waiting for our help.

We need more compassionate individuals like you to join in our work. If you make a commitment to joining PETA's Investigations & Rescue Fund—and support the fearless investigators who are uncovering abuse and rescuing animals—I will make a commitment to you. The donation you make will go directly toward supporting future investigations and rescues just like those described in this book.

Please consider protecting the most vulnerable animals. If you are ready to join PETA's Investigations & Rescue Fund team, you can sign up at **PETA.org/ Rescued**.

Thank you for taking the time to read this book. But most of all, thank you for being a friend to animals who are in desperate need of our respect and compassion.

—Ingrid